RECIPES FOR **SELF-LOVE**

HOW TO FEEL GOOD IN A PATRIARCHAL WORLD ♥ ALISON RACHEL

MORROW
GIFT
AN IMPRINT OF WILLIAM MORROW

KNOW YOUR WORTH

INTRODUCTION

I STARTED *RECIPES FOR SELF-LOVE* AS AN ATTEMPT TO CUT THROUGH THE NEGATIVE AND UNTRUE MEDIA THAT WOMEN AND TRANSFEMININE PEOPLE ARE EXPOSED TO EVERY DAY, MEDIA THAT TELLS US WE ARE WRONG AND SELLS US WHAT AND HOW WE'RE SUPPOSED TO BE. OVER THE YEARS, I HAVE DISCOVERED SOME TRUTHS THAT HAVE HELPED ME LIVE A MORE FREE LIFE—TRUTHS THAT ARE OUT THERE, THAT I BELIEVE WE MAY NATURALLY KNOW, BUT WHICH WE HAVE PERHAPS FORGOTTEN OR BEEN CONVINCED TO DISBELIEVE. THIS LITTLE BOOK, I HOPE, WILL SERVE AS A REMINDER THAT THERE IS NO ONE WAY TO LIVE OR BE, AND THAT WE WRITE OUR OWN MANIFESTOS FOR WHO WE ARE. HOPEFULLY IT WILL PROVIDE YOU WITH MOMENTS IN WHICH YOU CAN FIND TRIUMPH AND EMANCIPATION. MY AIM IS NOT TO BE IN ANY WAY PRESCRIPTIVE; I'M NOT A MENTAL HEALTH PROFESSIONAL, JUST SIMPLY AN ORDINARY PERSON WHO SEEKS TO SHARE SOME IDEAS THAT I HAVE FOUND LIBERATING.

WE ARE SO OFTEN CONCERNED WITH WHAT OTHER PEOPLE WILL THINK OF US THAT WE WILL FREQUENTLY GO OUT OF OUR WAY NOT TO OFFEND OR HURT OTHERS AT COST TO OURSELVES. WE WILL SPEAK QUIETER, SHRINK OUR-SELVES, ACT SUBMISSIVELY, OR OVERLY CHEERFUL IN ORDER TO GAIN APPROVAL WE THINK WE NEED OR TO AVOID CONFLICT, WHEN ULTIMATELY THE SITUATION IS CREATING STRESS FOR US. DON'T FEEL GUILTY ABOUT WANTING TO REMOVE YOURSELF FROM A SITUATION OR THE COMPANY OF PEOPLE WHO ARE DRAIN-ING YOUR ENERGY OR PUTTING STRAIN ON YOU.

PROTECT YOUR ENERGY

DON'T BE AFRAID TO LET GO OF TOXIC PEOPLE

THERE WILL BE PEOPLE IN YOUR LIFE THAT CAUSE YOU ANXIETY, THAT STRESS YOU OUT, AND WHO CONTRIBUTE TO YOUR UNHAPPINESS. THESE PEOPLE AREN'T ALWAYS AWARE OF THEIR EFFECT ON YOU AND MAY NOT BE WILLING TO ALTER THEIR ATTITUDE OR BEHAVIOR TOWARD YOU, EVEN WHEN CONFRONTED. YOU MAY NEED TO TAKE RESPONSIBILITY FOR THE NEGATIVE ENERGY THEY BRING INTO YOUR LIFE IF THEY WON'T. IF YOU DON'T THINK THERE IS A CHANCE OF RESOLVING THE SITUATION TOGETHER, IT MAY BE BEST TO REMOVE THE PERSON FROM YOUR LIFE. YOUR ENERGY IS PRECIOUS, TO BE USED FOR THINGS THAT ARE PRODUCTIVE AND FRUITFUL. DON'T LET IT BE DEPLETED BY TOXIC RELATIONSHIPS.

ALTHOUGH IT SOMETIMES IS DIFFICULT, TAKING THE OCCASIONAL BREAK FROM YOUR COMMITMENTS LIKE WORK OR SCHOOL IS VERY NECESSARY. IN ORDER TO DO YOUR BEST, YOU NEED TO BE MOTIVATED AND IF YOUR MOTIVATION IS LOW IT MAY BE A SIGN THAT YOU NEED TO TAKE SOME TIME OFF TO RECOVER YOUR ENERGY. WHEN YOU RETURN, YOU'LL HAVE A NEW SENSE OF VITALITY AND FEEL MORE INSPIRED.

REMEMBER TO TAKE TIME OFF

AS CHILDREN WE'RE OFTEN ASKED THE QUESTION BY ADULTS "WHAT DO YOU WANT TO BE WHEN YOU GROW UP?" WHAT THEY MEAN BY THIS IS *WHAT JOB DO YOU WANT TO HAVE?* USUALLY, THE MORE AMBITIOUS THE ANSWER THE MORE IMPRESSED THE ADULT.

CAPITALISM VALUES PRODUCTIVITY AND OUTPUT ABOVE ALL ELSE, AND AS WE ARE RAISED IN THIS SYSTEM WE ARE INDOCTRINATED BY IT. WE TEND TO SEE OURSELVES AND OTHERS AS MORE VALUABLE THE MORE SUCCESSFUL WE/THEY ARE. IF YOU GET A LOT OF THINGS DONE IN A DAY, YOU FEEL GOOD, AND SOMETIMES IF YOU SPEND THE WHOLE DAY LYING ON THE COUCH, YOU FEEL BAD. THIS IS AN EFFECT OF LIVING IN A CAPITALIST WORLD THAT PROJECTS THE IDEA THAT THE MORE PRODUCTIVE YOU ARE, THE MORE WORTH YOU HAVE, WHICH OF COURSE IS NOT TRUE. THIS IS NOT TO SAY THAT BEING AMBITIOUS IS A BAD THING, BUT IT'S IMPORTANT TO REMEMBER THAT YOU ARE MORE THAN YOUR OUTPUT AND ACHIEVEMENTS. YOU ARE IMPORTANT AND VALUABLE BECAUSE YOU ARE ALIVE RIGHT HERE AND NOW.

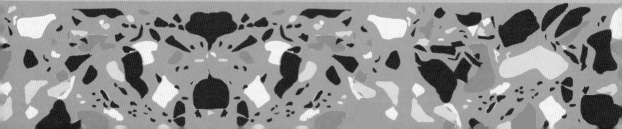

LIVING IN A CAPITALIST WORLD CAN LEAD
TO ANXIETY AND DEPRESSION

YOU'RE NOT GOING TO BE EVERYONE'S CUP OF TEA, BUT IT DOESN'T MATTER: THERE WILL BE OTHERS IN THIS WORLD THAT YOU CONNECT WITH SO DEEPLY IT MAKES THE HAIRS ON THE BACK OF YOUR NECK STAND UP. DON'T CHANGE YOURSELF IN ORDER TO GET OTHERS' APPROVAL AND DON'T FEEL THE NEED TO APOLOGIZE FOR WHO YOU ARE.

DON'T APOLOGIZE FOR WHO YOU ARE

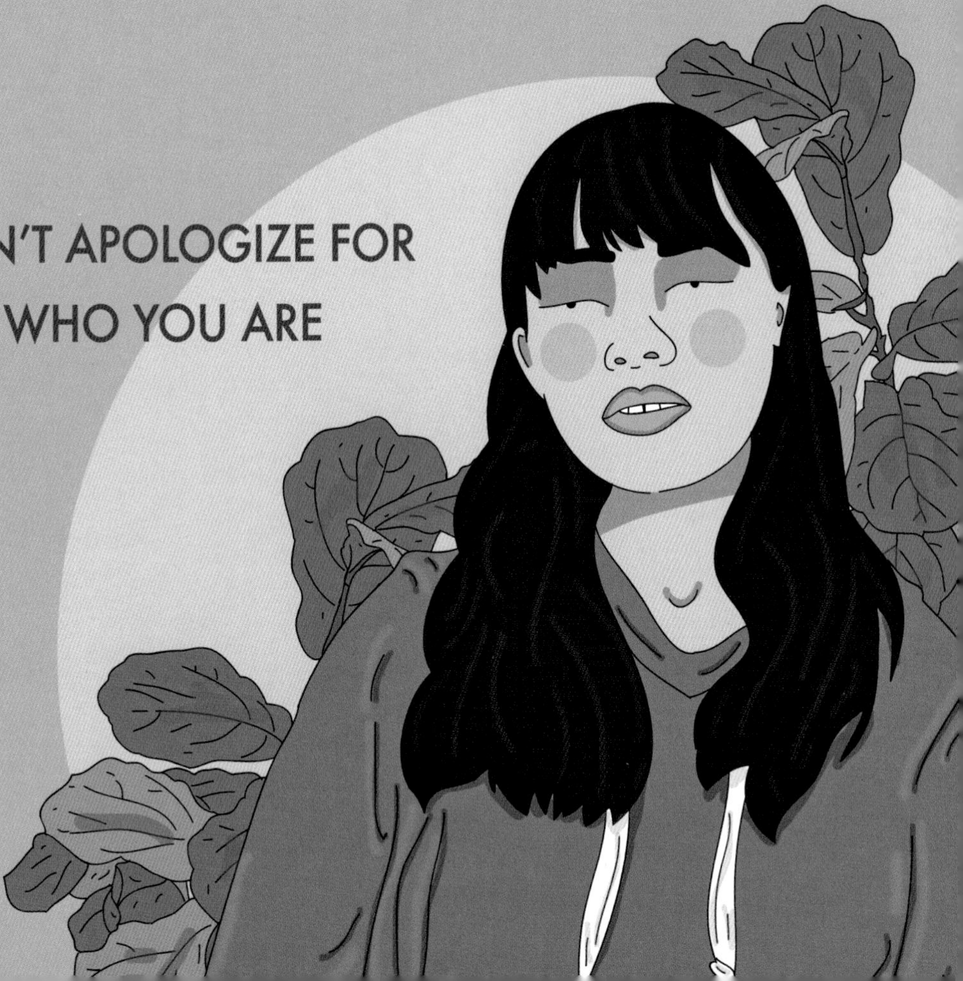

TAKE CARE OF YOURSELF

SELF-CARE COMES IN MANY DIFFERENT FORMS AND LOOKS DIFFERENT TO DIFFERENT PEOPLE. SOME CARE FOR THEMSELVES BY BEING PHYSICALLY ACTIVE WHILE OTHERS CARE FOR THEMSELVES BY DOING THE OPPOSITE AND SPENDING THE DAY IN BED WITH A BOOK OR MOVIE. WHETHER IT'S EATING A NUTRITIOUS MEAL OR A DELICIOUS PIECE OF CAKE, GOING FOR A LONG RUN OR HAVING A LONG INTROSPECTIVE SESSION OF SELF-ASSESSMENT, WHATEVER YOU NEED TO DO TO TAKE CARE OF YOURSELF . . . DO IT.

SOMETIMES YOU JUST NEED TO HIDE FROM
THE WORLD

YOU DON'T ALWAYS NEED TO SHOW A BRAVE FACE OR FORCE YOURSELF TO BE STRONG. ALTHOUGH THOSE THINGS ARE IMPORTANT, THERE ARE TIMES WHEN ALL YOU WANT TO DO IS CURL UP IN BED AND HIDE FROM THE WORLD. WHEN LIFE JUST SEEMS TOO MUCH TO BEAR AND YOU JUST WANT TO ESCAPE IT ALL FOR A WHILE, TAKE SOME TIME OUT, REST, AND SPEND THE DAY BEING GENTLE TO YOURSELF. IT'S IMPORTANT.

DON'T CONCERN YOURSELF WITH WHAT OTHERS THINK OF YOU

THIS CAN BE A VERY DIFFICULT THING TO DO, BUT IT'S SO LIBERATING TO LET GO OF HOW OTHERS ARE JUDGING YOU. THERE WILL ALWAYS BE PEOPLE WHO DON'T UNDERSTAND YOU AND WHY YOU DO WHAT YOU DO. DON'T BOTHER TOO MUCH WITH PEOPLE LIKE THAT. LEARN TO TRUST YOURSELF AND HOW YOU FEEL ABOUT WHO YOU ARE. STAY FOCUSED ON YOUR GOALS AND WHAT YOU WANT TO GET OUT OF LIFE. ULTIMATELY, ACHIEVING THESE THINGS WILL BE MORE SATISFYING THAN ANYONE ELSE'S STAMP OF APPROVAL.

SO MANY THINGS CONTRIBUTE TO YOU BEING YOU. LIKE A MULTIFACETED DIAMOND, YOU REFLECT AND REFRACT DIFFERENT COLORS IN LIGHT. YOU CAN ENJOY WATCHING BAD REALITY TELEVISION OR SOAP OPERAS AND ALSO BE A DEEPLY SPIRITUAL PERSON; YOU CAN BE INTO NERDY SUBCULTURES AND ALSO ENJOY PARTYING HARD. TRY NOT TO LIMIT YOURSELF OR SUBSCRIBE TOO STRICTLY TO ANY CHARACTERISTICS OF A CULTURE OR SUBCULTURE YOU IDENTIFY WITH. FEEL FREE TO EXPLORE AND EXPRESS ALL THE DIFFERENT YOUS THAT EXIST.

YOU ARE MULTIFACETED AND MULTIDIMENSIONAL

ITS OKAY TO NOT BE OKAY

YOU DON'T HAVE TO BE OKAY ALL THE TIME. YOU'RE ALLOWED TO BE UPSET, TO BE A MESS, AND TO BE TOTALLY NOT OKAY. LIFE IS MESSY AND UNPREDICTABLE; IT THROWS YOU CURVE BALLS THAT YOU'RE NOT ALWAYS GOING TO KNOW HOW TO HANDLE. THERE IS NO SHAME IN NOT BEING OKAY.

YOU DON'T ALWAYS HAVE TO BE HAPPY

IT'S UNREALISTIC TO EXPECT YOURSELF TO SUSTAIN CONTENTMENT AND HAPPINESS EVERYDAY; IT'S NOT ONLY IMPOSSIBLE BUT ALSO UNNATURAL. EVEN IN NATURE LIVING THINGS DON'T PRODUCE ALL YEAR ROUND; THEY HIBERNATE, TAKE A BREAK, SHRINK UP, AND SAVE ENERGY FOR THE NEXT SEASON OF PRODUCTIVITY. WE ARE NO DIFFERENT. WE GO THROUGH SEASONS, AND SOMETIMES THOSE SEASONS ARE HARD OR UNPLEASANT OR FULL OF SADNESS.

BEING HONEST ABOUT FEELING UNHAPPY SOMETIMES CAN MAKE OTHER PEOPLE UNCOMFORTABLE BECAUSE SADNESS IS SEEN AS SOMETHING NEGATIVE. THEY MAY WANT TO CHEER YOU UP, OR TELL YOU NOT TO FEEL SORRY FOR YOURSELF OR BE SO DOWN. YOU DON'T HAVE TO HAVE AN EXPLANATION FOR WHY YOU ARE FEELING UNHAPPY—SOMETIMES THERE IS NO REASON. BE HONEST WITH YOURSELF ABOUT HOW YOU FEEL, ESPECIALLY WHEN YOU'RE FEELING DOWN OR EXPERIENCING A LOW MOOD. DON'T BE HARD ON YOURSELF, AND REMEMBER THAT LIFE IS FULL OF UPS AND DOWNS SO ALLOW YOURSELF TO BE HAPPY, ALLOW YOURSELF TO BE MISERABLE, AND EVERYTHING IN BETWEEN.

SURROUND YOURSELF WITH PEOPLE WHO ADD
VALUE TO YOUR LIFE

LIFE IS SO FULL OF SPECIAL BONDS AND FRIENDSHIPS LIKE THOSE SHARED WITH PALS, FAMILY, MENTORS, ROMANTIC PARTNERS, AND EVEN PEOPLE YOU DON'T KNOW PARTICULARLY WELL. TRY TO SURROUND YOURSELF WITH THOSE PEOPLE THAT REALLY ADD VALUE TO YOUR LIFE, AND DON'T FORGET ABOUT WHAT VALUE YOU ADD TO THE LIVES OF OTHERS. SPEND TIME AND ENERGY INVESTING IN THESE REMARKABLE RELATIONSHIPS SO THEY WILL GROW AND LAST.

DON'T FEEL GUILTY ABOUT PUTTING
YOURSELF FIRST

IT'S DIFFICULT TO BE YOUR BEST SELF IF YOU AREN'T FEELING LIKE YOURSELF. SELF-PRESERVATION IS SO IMPORTANT AND SOMETIMES IN LIFE YOU NEED TO PUT YOURSELF FIRST TO ENSURE THAT YOU'RE GETTING WHAT YOU NEED. PRIORITIZING YOUR OWN NEEDS WHEN IT'S NECESSARY DOESN'T MEAN YOU'RE A SELFISH OR BAD PERSON; IT JUST MEANS YOU'RE TAKING CARE OF YOURSELF, WHICH WILL ULTIMATELY HELP YOU GIVE MORE TO OTHERS.

SAYING NO CAN TAKE SOME PRACTICE. WE SO OFTEN DON'T WANT TO DIS-APPOINT OR HURT PEOPLE AND THINK THAT SAYING "NO" TO THEM MIGHT DO JUST THAT. BEING A "YES" PERSON HAS MANY BENEFITS, BUT BOUNDARY SETTING IS ALSO IMPORTANT. REMEMBER THAT YOU CAN'T CONTROL OTHER PEOPLE'S FEELINGS AND CANNOT BE HELD RESPONSIBLE IF YOUR BOUNDARY SETTING ISN'T FOUND TO BE AGREEABLE BY OTHERS. IF THEY CARE ABOUT YOU, THEY WILL UNDERSTAND WHEN YOU HAVE TO SAY NO.

IT'S OKAY TO SAY "NO"

QUITTING DOESN'T ALWAYS EQUATE FAILURE

SOMETIMES QUITTING CAN MEAN THE COMPLETE OPPOSITE OF FAILURE; SOME-
TIMES IT CAN MARK A SUCCESS. QUITTING OFTEN TAKES COURAGE, WISDOM,
AND STRENGTH—IT ALSO TAKES HONESTY TO KNOW WHEN SOMETHING ISN'T
WORKING AND TO KNOW WHEN THE TIME IS RIGHT TO MOVE ON TO SOME-
THING ELSE.

NEVER FEEL GUILTY ABOUT YOUR FEELINGS

WE TEND TO JUDGE OUR EMOTIONS AND CATEGORIZE THEM AS EITHER GOOD OR BAD. WE ALSO OFTEN FULLY IDENTIFY WITH THE UNPLEASANT FEELINGS WE EXPERIENCE WHEN WE DON'T HAVE TO. THERE IS NO SUCH THING AS A "BAD" EMOTION OR FEELING. ALL YOUR FEELINGS ARE REAL AND VALID AND IMPORTANT, THE POSITIVE AS WELL AS THE NEGATIVE. YOU DON'T ALWAYS HAVE TO BE HAPPY AND STRONG. ALLOW YOURSELF TO PROCESS ALL EMOTIONS FULLY, ESPECIALLY FEELINGS OF SADNESS, SORROW, MISERY, ANGER, AND OTHERS CONSIDERED TO BE "BAD." DON'T FORCE YOURSELF OR OTHERS TO BE POSITIVE IF AND WHEN THEY'RE FEELING DOWN. RATHER, TRY TO SIMPLY REMAIN LOVING AND PRESENT. LEARNING HOW TO SURVIVE DISCOMFORT AND PAIN WILL HELP YOU GROW AND TO MORE FULLY EXPERIENCE JOY, PLEASURE, AND CONTENTMENT WHEN THEY ARISE.

WE ARE ALL OUT HERE JUST TRYING TO DO OUR BEST AND BE OUR BEST, BUT IT'S IMPOSSIBLE NOT TO BE SCATHED BY THE UPS AND DOWNS OF LIFE. THESE KNOCKS OFTEN LEAVE BRUISES AND SCARS AND MAKE US SCARED TO TRY AGAIN OR MOVE FORWARD. IT'S NORMAL AND NATURAL TO BE CAUTIOUS AND WANT TO PROTECT YOURSELF FROM PAIN. HOWEVER, THIS SELF-PROTECTION DOES SOMETIMES HOLD US BACK AND CAN INHIBIT US FROM LIVING LIFE FULLY. IT TAKES TIME TO HEAL AND BECOME A PERSON CAPABLE OF GIVING AND RE-CEIVING MORE LOVE. YOU DO WANT TO HEAL, YOU DO WANT TO BE HAPPY AND WHOLE, BUT YOU MUST BE PATIENT WITH YOURSELF; IT'S NOT GOING TO HAPPEN OVERNIGHT.

BE PATIENT WITH YOURSELF

YOU ARE NOT ALONE

THE INDIVIDUALISM OF WESTERN SOCIETY LEADS US TO BELIEVE THAT WE ARE ALL SEPARATE FROM ONE ANOTHER, WHEN THE TRUTH IS THAT WE ARE ALL CONNECTED. TRY TO REMEMBER THAT YOU ARE EXPERIENCING LIFE ALONG WITH BILLIONS OF OTHER PEOPLE, MANY OF WHOM ARE LIVING THROUGH THE SAME THINGS AS YOU AND FEELING THE SAME WAY. SEE THIS AS AN OPPORTUNITY TO REACH OUT TO OTHERS AROUND YOU AND CONNECT ON A DEEPER LEVEL THAN YOU USUALLY WOULD. THIS WILL LEAD YOU TO FIND A COMMUNITY OF PEOPLE WHO FEEL THE SAME WAY AS YOU DO OR WHO ARE GOING THROUGH SIMILAR EXPERIENCES.

THERE IS PAIN IN GROWTH AND GROWTH IN PAIN. THE TWO OFTEN GO HAND IN HAND. YOU CANNOT KNOW THE FULL RICHNESS OF JOY, PLEASURE, AND CONTENTMENT IF YOU HAVEN'T EXPERIENCED EMOTIONAL PAIN AND SADNESS. THIS ISN'T TO ROMANTICIZE PAIN IN ANY WAY, BUT TO SAY THAT PAIN CAN OFTEN BE A GOOD TEACHER AND HELP YOU DEVELOP AND GROW IN NEW WAYS. PAIN OF ANY KIND, OF COURSE, CAN BE VERY UNPLEASANT, AND WE ARE BIOLOGICALLY PROGRAMMED TO AVOID IT AND SEEK COMFORT. BUT IF YOU CAN, LEAN INTO YOUR EMOTIONAL PAIN, WRESTLE WITH IT, AND LEARN FROM IT. YOU WILL WITHOUT A DOUBT EMERGE FROM YOUR PAIN A WISER PERSON. ACKNOWLEDGE THAT PAIN IS A PART OF YOU, AND MAYBE ALWAYS WILL BE. SEE IF YOU CAN REALIZE THE WISDOM AND DEPTH GAINED FROM TIMES OF DISCOMFORT.

DON'T LET THE PAIN OF GROWTH
INHIBIT YOUR GROWTH

SPEAK KINDLY TO YOURSELF

WORDS ARE SUCH POWERFUL THINGS. THEY'RE IMPORTANT AND MAKE A DIF-FERENCE EVEN WHEN YOU DON'T THINK THAT THEY DO. PAY ATTENTION TO THE KIND OF LANGUAGE YOU USE WHEN YOU SPEAK TO AND ABOUT YOURSELF. WE SOMETIMES GET INTO THE HABIT OF NEGATIVE SELF-TALK, SELF-DEPRECATION, AND PUTTING OURSELVES DOWN BECAUSE WE THINK IT WILL MAKE US MORE RELATABLE OR LIKEABLE. THESE ARE BAD HABITS AND ALTHOUGH THEY MAY SEEM HARMLESS, THEY CAN BECOME DANGEROUS IF THEY BECOME YOUR DEFAULT. RATHER, PRACTICE SPEAKING KINDLY TO YOURSELF AND POSITIVELY ABOUT YOURSELF.

CIS-GENDERED MEN WILL NEVER EXPERIENCE SEXISM; THEY HAVE NEVER BEEN SYSTEMICALLY DISENFRANCHISED, OR SUBJUGATED BY WOMEN. BECAUSE THEY'VE NEVER EXPERIENCED SEXISM, IT FOLLOWS THAT THEY WON'T BE ABLE TO IDENTIFY IT AS CLEARLY AS A PERSON WHO ACTUALLY DOES EXPERIENCE IT. THIS LOGIC SUPPORTS THE IDEA THAT MEN NEVER GET TO DECIDE WHAT IS OR WHAT ISN'T SEXIST AND SHOULD ALWAYS BELIEVE A WOMAN WHEN SHE IDENTIFIES SOMETHING AS SEXIST. SIMILARLY, WHITE PEOPLE DO NOT GET TO DECIDE WHAT IS RACIST, AND ABLE-BODIED PEOPLE WHAT IS ABLEIST, ETC., ETC. IF YOU ARE A PART OF THE DOMINANT POWER STRUCTURE, YOU DON'T GET TO MAKE JUDGE-MENTS ABOUT OPPRESSED PEOPLES' LIVED EXPERIENCES. IT'S IMPORTANT FOR PEOPLE WITH MALE/WHITE/CIS, ETC. PRIVILEGE TO LISTEN CAREFULLY TO THOSE WHO SUFFER FROM SYSTEMIC OPPRESSION AND DO WHAT THEY CAN TO INTER-ROGATE THEIR RELATION TO POWER AND THE EFFECTS OF IT.

MEN DON'T GET TO DECIDE WHAT IS SEXIST

WE LIVE IN A WORLD THAT HIGHLY ESTEEMS GOOD LOOKS. THE MORE A PERSON ADHERES TO BEAUTY STANDARDS THE MORE SOCIETY VALUES THEM. SINCE "BEAUTY" IS A SOCIAL CONSTRUCT THAT VARIES DEPENDING ON TIME PERIOD AND LOCATION, IT SEEMS BIZARRE TO APPLY SUCH A STANDARD IN THE FIRST PLACE, NOT TO MENTION ASSIGN WORTH TO PEOPLE BASED ON THIS RIDICULOUS CRITERIA.

THIS VALUE SYSTEM DISPROPORTIONATELY AFFECTS WOMEN AND TRANSFEMININE PEOPLE, AND ALTHOUGH MEN ARE ALSO JUDGED BY HOW THEY LOOK, THEY CAN STILL EASILY BECOME HIGHLY SUCCESSFUL PEOPLE SOCIALLY, ECONOMICALLY, AND POLITICALLY DESPITE NOT BEING CONSIDERED CONVENTIONALLY GOOD-LOOKING. IT'S A LOT MORE DIFFICULT FOR EVERYONE ELSE TO NAVIGATE THEIR WAY THROUGH THE WORLD IF THEY DON'T HAVE "PRETTY PRIVILEGE." THIS IS BECAUSE SOCIETY VALUES MEN FOR THEIR INTELLECT AND ABILITIES AND NOT PURELY THEIR LOOKS. FOR EVERYONE ELSE, IT'S A DIFFERENT STORY. OUR PERCEIVED VALUE IS CLOSELY LINKED TO THE WAY OUR BODIES LOOK. IF WE ARE CONSIDERED "PRETTY" AND ADHERE TO BEAUTY STANDARDS, WE ARE LARGELY VIEWED AS MORE VALUABLE AS PEOPLE.

CONTINUED

YOUR BODY IS NOT A
REFLECTION OF YOUR WORTH

THE TRUTH IS YOU ARE SO MUCH MORE THAN YOUR BODY AND THE WAY YOU LOOK. TRY TO UNLEARN YOUR INTERNALIZED SEXISM AND THOSE CONCEPTS OF EQUATING THE WAY YOU LOOK TO YOUR VALUE. REMAIN CONSCIOUS OF HOW YOUR PRESENCE ON THIS EARTH IS INCREDIBLE AND SPECIAL, THAT YOU HAVE SO MUCH TO EXPERIENCE AND SO MUCH TO GIVE. YOU ARE UNIQUE, THE ONLY YOU THAT HAS EVER EXISTED AND WHO EVER WILL, AND YOU ARE SO VERY IMPORTANT THE WAY YOU ARE.

HAVE YOUR GIRL'S BACK

ONE OF THE MOST SUCCESSFUL LIES THE MEDIA SELLS WOMEN IS THAT WE ARE EACH OTHER'S COMPETITION OR THAT WE ALL NEED TO BE THE SAME. THIS IDEA IS PERPETUATED BY THE SOCIETAL STANDARD OF BEAUTY, WHICH PITS US AGAINST EACH OTHER FOR THE APPROVAL OF MEN. THIS COMPETITION ALSO SERVES AS AN ATTEMPT TO SEPARATE US FROM ONE ANOTHER, BECAUSE WE ARE STRONGER WHEN WE ARE TOGETHER, AND IF WE'RE BUSY TEARING EACH OTHER DOWN WE CAN'T UNITE TO FIGHT THE PATRIARCHY. SO MUCH WON-DERFUL DIVERSITY EXISTS AMONGST WOMEN AND TRANSFEMININE PEOPLE, AND THERE EXIST SO MANY DIFFERENT EXPERIENCES AMONG US. ONE SHOULD LISTEN AND LEARN FROM OTHERS AND SUPPORT THEM, ESPECIALLY WOMEN/ FEMMES/GENDER-NONCONFORMING FOLKS WHO ARE DIFFERENT FROM YOU; IT'S FROM THEM YOU HAVE THE MOST TO LEARN.

SUPPORT THOSE WHO ARE
DIFFERENT FROM YOU

DON'T BE AFRAID TO ASK FOR HELP

IT CAN BE INCREDIBLY DIFFICULT TO DEAL WITH THE CHALLENGES LIFE THROWS AT YOU WHEN YOU'RE ON YOUR OWN. WE'RE GENERALLY TOLD IT'S GOOD TO BE SELF-RELIANT AND INDEPENDENT, AND ALTHOUGH IT DOES FEEL GOOD TO BE SELF-SUFFICIENT, THERE ARE TIMES WHEN WE CANNOT MANAGE ON OUR OWN AND COULD REALLY USE A HELPING HAND. BE SPECIFIC ABOUT WHO YOU WANT TO ASK FOR HELP AND THE KIND OF HELP YOU NEED. DON'T BE AFRAID TO ASK FOR HELP WHEN YOU FEEL LIKE YOU'RE STRUGGLING. THERE IS NO SHAME IN ADMITTING THAT YOU NEED A HAND. TRY ALSO TO BE SENSITIVE TO THE PEOPLE YOU CARE ABOUT WHEN THEY MAY BE UNDER STRAIN AND NEED SOME EXTRA SUPPORT.

WE ARE COMPLEX BEINGS, MADE UP OF INTERNAL AND EXTERNAL ASPECTS; THE PHYSICAL, PSYCHOLOGICAL, EMOTIONAL, AND SPIRITUAL. WE NEED TO LOOK AFTER ALL PARTS OF OURSELVES AND NOT NEGLECT ONE OR THE OTHERS. PAY ATTENTION TO HOW YOU TAKE CARE OF YOUR PHYSICAL SELF, WHETHER YOU'RE GETTING ENOUGH SLEEP OR STAYING HYDRATED. IF SOMETHING IS OUT OF WHACK IT MIGHT THROW YOU OFF AND INHIBIT YOU FROM LIVING YOUR BEST LIFE. THE SAME GOES FOR YOUR EMOTIONAL AND SPIRITUAL SELVES. ARE YOU GETTING WHAT YOU NEED TO MAINTAIN A BALANCE IN ALL AREAS OF YOUR LIFE? IF YOU'RE NOT, IT'S TOTALLY OKAY—WE SELDOM ARE IN A PLACE WHERE WE'RE TOTALLY HAPPY WITH ALL ASPECTS OF OURSELVES. BUT TAKING CARE OF YOURSELF IS A VALUABLE AND HELPFUL THING TO BE MINDFUL OF AT ALL TIMES. PRACTICE CHECKING IN WITH YOURSELF ONCE OR TWICE A WEEK—EVEN MORE OFTEN IF YOU CAN—ASKING YOURSELF HOW YOU'RE FEELING AND TAKE STOCK OF YOUR ENERGY LEVELS, BOTH PHYSICAL AND EMOTIONAL.

CHECK IN WITH YOURSELF

THE IDEA OF A STANDARD OF BEAUTY—UNREALISTIC IDEALS FOR WOMEN AND FEMMES PERTAINING TO LOOKS AND BEHAVIOR—WAS INVENTED BY WHAT AUTHOR BELL HOOKS CALLS THE WHITE-SUPREMACIST-CAPITALIST-PATRIARCHY TO CONTROL AND OPPRESS US. BY ENFORCING THE NOTION THAT THERE IS AN "IDEAL" WAY TO LOOK OR BE, WE ARE PERSUADED TO SPEND OUR TIME, ENERGY, AND MONEY ON TRYING TO FIX OUR "FLAWS" RATHER THAN ON OTHER POSSIBLY MORE IMPORTANT THINGS LIKE EDUCATION, CAREERS, OR OTHER GOALS. THE WHITE-SUPREMACIST-CAPITALIST-PATRIARCHY BENEFITS LARGELY FROM US HATING OURSELVES, NOT ONLY BECAUSE IT CONTRIBUTES TO THE ECONOMY WHEN WE SPEND MONEY ON CHANGING OR "IMPROVING" OUR-SELVES, BUT IT ALSO MINIMIZES THE COMPETITION FOR CIS MEN IN THE WORK PLACE AND OTHER INSTITUTIONS.

BEAUTY IDEALS HAVE CHANGED OVER THE YEARS AND ARE CONSTANTLY EVOLVING, AND MANY WOMEN ARE ALREADY WORKING HARD TO INTERROGATE AND DISMANTLE THESE IDEALS. TRY TO BE CRITICAL OF THE UNREALISTIC BEAUTY STANDARDS YOU SEE AROUND YOU AND ALSO OF THE ONES YOU HAVE INTERNALIZED.

TIP. GET YOURSELF A COPY OF NAOMI WOLF'S *THE BEAUTY MYTH* AND FAMILIARIZE YOURSELF WITH THE WORK OF BELL HOOKS, WHO WRITES EXTENSIVELY ON THIS TOPIC.

BEAUTY IS A CONSTRUCT

WE SO OFTEN HOLD OURSELVES TO IMPOSSIBLE STANDARDS AND COME DOWN HARD ON OURSELVES. YOU'VE HEARD THE PLATITUDE "NOBODY'S PERFECT," BUT PERHAPS WHAT YOU HAVEN'T HEARD BEFORE IS THAT THERE IS SO MUCH MORE RICHNESS IN A LIFE THAT IS FILLED WITH UPS AND DOWNS, STRUGGLES AND VICTORIES, MISTAKES AND FORGIVENESS. IT'S TRUE THAT NOBODY IS PERFECT, BUT IT'S ALSO TRUE THAT OUR FLAWS MAKE WAY FOR GROWTH AND WISDOM. DON'T LET THE SHAME OF YOUR PAST MISTAKES HOLD YOU BACK FROM WHAT THEY WERE MEANT TO DO: TEACH YOU SOMETHING. FORGIVE YOURSELF.

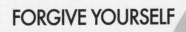

FORGIVE YOURSELF

SKIN IS A FEMINIST ISSUE

THERE IS ALWAYS SO MUCH PRESSURE ON US TO HAVE CLEAR SKIN. EVERYONE'S BODY IS DIFFERENT, AND JUST LIKE SOME BODIES ARE FAT AND SOME ARE THIN, SOME PEOPLE ARE PRONE TO OILY SKIN OR ACNE. THIS TOPIC IS SELDOM SPOKEN ABOUT WITHIN BODY-POSITIVE DISCOURSE AND PEOPLE WITH "BAD SKIN" ARE HEAVILY UNDERREPRESENTED IN THE MEDIA; AND IF THEY ARE REPRESENTED, IT'S USUALLY NOT IN A GOOD WAY. SIMILAR TO FAT SHAMING, PEOPLE MAKE UNREASONABLE JUDGMENTS ABOUT THOSE WHO HAVE ACNE—FOR EXAMPLE, ASSUMING THEY'RE DIRTY OR EAT BADLY. PEOPLE ARE SOMETIMES INSENSITIVE, EXPECTING THOSE WITH ACNE TO SEEK OUT OFTEN EXPENSIVE TREATMENTS THAT MANY DON'T HAVE ACCESS TO. TRY TO UNLEARN THE ASSUMPTIONS YOU HAVE ABOUT ACNE AND OTHER SKIN CONDITIONS CONSIDERED TO BE "BAD." DON'T HATE PEOPLE WITH PIMPLES, SPOTS, MARKS, PSORIASIS, DISCOLORATION, AND SCARS, WHICH DO NOT EQUAL BAD SKIN!

WEAR WHAT MAKES YOU FEEL GOOD

CLOTHING CAN BE AN IMPORTANT EXPRESSION OF IDENTITY, BUT ONE THAT CAN ALSO BE CHALLENGING WHEN GOING OUT IN PUBLIC DUE TO CIS-HETERO NORMATIVITY AND THE PATRIARCHAL WORLD WE LIVE IN. PRACTICE BEING MORE CONSCIOUS OF WEARING WHAT MAKES YOU FEEL GOOD. DRESS MASCULINE OR SUPER FEMININE, COVER UP OR SHOW A LOT OF YOUR BODY. ROCK HIGH HEELS, GO BAREFOOT, WEAR LOADS OF MAKEUP, OR NONE AT ALL. IF TIGHT CLOTHES MAKE YOU FEEL GOOD OR LOOSE CLOTHES MAKE YOU FEEL MORE COMFORTABLE, DO WHATEVER YOU WANT TO HELP YOU FEEL MOST LIKE YOUR-SELF WHEN NAVIGATING THE WORLD.

OTHER WOMEN ARE NOT YOUR COMPETITION

THE PATRIARCHAL SOCIETY WE LIVE IN TEACHES WOMEN AND GIRLS TO SEE EACH OTHER AS COMPETITORS. COMPETITORS FOR ATTENTION, BEAUTY, AND SUCCESS. BECAUSE OF THE BEAUTY STANDARDS THAT EXIST, WE ARE CONSTANTLY COMPARING OURSELVES TO EACH OTHER TO SEE HOW WE EACH MEASURE UP TO SAID STANDARDS. THIS IS A BIZARRE PRACTICE SINCE THESE BEAUTY STANDARDS ARE TOTALLY ARBITRARY, AND ALSO BECAUSE COMPETING WITH OTHER WOMEN WILL NOT FURTHER OUR CAUSE TO DISMANTLE THE SYSTEM THAT PITS US AGAINST EACH OTHER IN THE FIRST PLACE. TRY TO UNLEARN SEEING OTHER WOMEN/FEMMES AS YOUR COMPETITION. REFLECT ON HOW YOU ARE TOTALLY UNIQUE AND COULDN'T EVEN BEGIN TO BE COMPARED TO ANYONE ELSE. THEN TRY TO PRACTICE BUILDING OTHER WOMEN UP AND WHEN YOU SEE THEM THRIVING, THINK ABOUT HOW THAT BENEFITS YOU AS A WOMAN AND HOW EVERY TIME A WOMAN SUCCEEDS SHE MAKES IT EASIER FOR OTHER WOMEN TO FOLLOW HER LEAD AND DO THE SAME.

BODY HAIR IS NATURAL

THROUGHOUT HISTORY, FASHION, POPULAR CULTURE, AND—RECENTLY—PORN HAVE ALL CONTRIBUTED TO WOMEN BELIEVING THEIR BODY HAIR IS OBSCENE AND UNSIGHTLY. AS A RESULT, WOMEN SUFFER THROUGH THE PAIN OF WAXING, TWEEZING, RAZOR CUTS, INGROWN HAIRS, AND MORE, ALL TO BE MORE AESTHETICALLY CONSUMABLE FOR OTHERS. WE HAVE ALSO DEEPLY INTERNALIZED THE IDEA THAT OUR BODIES LOOK BETTER HAIRLESS FROM THE NECK DOWN AND OFTEN GENUINELY PREFER TO BE HAIRLESS. THERE IS NOTHING WRONG WITH REMOVING YOUR BODY HAIR IF THAT'S WHAT YOU PREFER—FEMINISM IS ABOUT FREEDOM OF CHOICE AND SUPPORTS WHATEVER YOU DECIDE TO DO WITH YOUR BODY. THAT BEING SAID, REMEMBER THAT BODY HAIR IS NATURAL AND THERE FOR A REASON, SO BE AWARE OF WHY IT IS YOU ARE CHOOSING TO/NOT TO REMOVE YOUR BODY HAIR.

A "REAL WOMAN" IS WHATEVER
SHE WANTS TO BE

THE MEDIA IS FULL OF PRESCRIPTIVE LANGUAGE ABOUT WHAT WOMEN ARE AND HOW THEY SHOULD BE. YOU'VE NO DOUBT HEARD TIRED TROPES ABOUT A REAL WOMAN HAVING CURVES OR A REAL WOMAN DOES THIS, THAT, OR THE OTHER. THIS IS, OF COURSE, NONSENSE, BECAUSE BEING A WOMAN IS NOT MONO-LITHIC, AND ANYONE WHO IDENTIFIES AS A WOMAN IS IN FACT A WOMAN, AND CAN BE ANY KIND OF PERSON SHE WISHES TO BE. MANY OF US BECOME SO BOGGED DOWN NEGOTIATING RESPECTABILITY POLITICS WE FORGET THAT WE DON'T NEED TO BEHAVE OR LOOK A CERTAIN WAY IN ORDER TO BE RE-SPECTED. REMEMBER THIS WHEN NEXT YOU COME INTO CONTACT WITH MEDIA OR A PERSON SPOUTING RHETORIC ABOUT HOW A "REAL WOMAN" SHOULD LOOK OR BEHAVE AND TRY TO DISRUPT IT.

THERE ARE MANY WAYS TO HAVE SEX THAT DON'T INCLUDE PENIS-IN-VAGINA. THIS MISCONCEPTION EXCLUDES A MYRIAD OF OTHER FORMS OF SEXUAL ACTS WHICH ARE VALID AND COUNT AS HAVING SEX. THIS LIMITED DEFINITION IS HETERONORMATIVE, AND ALSO CAN MINIMIZE THE EXPERIENCES OF SEXUAL ASSAULT SURVIVORS BY CALLING THEIR VICTIMIZATION INTO QUESTION IF THERE WAS NO ACTUAL PENETRATION.

THIS NARROW IDEA OF SEX IS ALSO USED TO CONTROL WOMEN'S SEXUALITY BECAUSE IT'S CLOSELY LINKED TO THE IDEA OF VIRGINITY, AN IDEA ESPOUSED BY MANY RELIGIONS AS A WAY OF CONTROLLING FEMALE SEXUALITY AND WHICH REGARDS WOMEN SIMPLY AS CHILDBEARERS AND PROPERTY. PSEUDOSCIENCE AND POPULAR CULTURE CREATED THE MYTH THAT AN INTACT HYMEN EQUATES TO VIRGINITY. VIRGINITY PERPETUATES THE IDEA THAT WOMAN ARE OBJECTS THAT DECREASE IN VALUE AFTER THEY HAVE HAD SEX, AS IF THEIR VIRGINITY BELONGS TO SOMEONE ELSE OR IS SOMETHING WHICH, ONCE LOST, RESULTS IN THE SUBJECT BEING TARNISHED. THESE RIDICULOUS NOTIONS SHOULD BE OUTRIGHT REJECTED BECAUSE WOMEN'S BODIES AND SEXUALITY BELONG TO THEM AND THEM ALONE, AND THEY CAN DO WITH THEM AS THEY PLEASE; THESE ACTIONS HAVE NO BEARING ON THEIR WORTH AS HUMAN BEINGS.

ALWAYS REMEMBER THAT SEX IS ABOUT PLEASURE, SO REGARDLESS OF WHO YOU'RE HAVING SEX WITH, YOU SHOULD BE HAVING FUN AND ENJOYING YOURSELF.

THERE IS MORE TO SEX THAN PENETRATION

DON'T MAKE FUN OF OTHER WOMEN/ FEMMES

AS PREVIOUSLY MENTIONED, WE HAVE LONG BEEN INDOCTRINATED BY THE PATRIARCHY TO BELIEVE THAT WOMEN ARE OUR COMPETITION. THIS STRATEGY KEEPS US FOCUSED ON BEING CRITICAL OF EACH OTHER RATHER THAN CHALLENGING THE DOMINANT POWER STRUCTURES THAT KEEP US SUBJUGATED. WE ARE SO USED TO BEING CRITICAL OF OTHER WOMEN—IT'S EASY TO SIT IN A PUBLIC PLACE AND JUST COMMENT CRITICALLY ON BODIES OR CHOICES OF CLOTHING. THIS IS A BAD HABIT, AND ONE THAT WE SHOULD ALL TRY TO BREAK. SOCIETY IS HIGHLY CRITICAL OF US; WE DON'T NEED TO BE AS WELL. DON'T MAKE FUN OF OTHER WOMEN OR FEMMES, DON'T COMMENT NEGATIVELY ON THEIR HAIR, THEIR FASHION, THEIR BODIES. DON'T SAY THEY'RE TOO YOUNG OR TOO OLD. OTHER WOMEN'S CHOICES TO EXPRESS THEMSELVES HAVE NOTHING TO DO WITH YOU AND BY COMMENTING NEGATIVELY YOU ARE BEING AN AGENT OF THE PATRIARCHY.

YOU'RE LEARNING MORE ABOUT YOURSELF ALL THE TIME. EVERY TIME YOU MAKE A CHOICE, AND RESPOND TO THE WORLD AROUND YOU (OR EVEN YOUR OWN INTERNAL THOUGHTS), YOU ARE LEARNING MORE ABOUT YOURSELF. THIS PROCESS IS SUCH A WONDERFUL AND PRECIOUS JOURNEY OF GROWTH. OTHER PEOPLE HAVE NO RIGHT TO GET IN THE WAY OF THIS. YOU ARE UNIQUE AND WONDERFUL, YOU DON'T NEED APPROVAL FROM ANYONE TO BE YOURSELF, SO DON'T HOLD BACK IN BEING CONFIDENT AND PROJECTING YOURSELF INTO THE WORLD.

YOU DON'T NEED PERMISSION TO BE YOURSELF

DESEXUALIZE WOMEN'S BODIES

WOMEN GO FROM BEING CHILDREN TO SEXUAL OBJECTS PRETTY QUICKLY; SOMETIMES THE LINE BETWEEN THE TWO IS EVEN BLURRED, WHAT WITH MINORS BEING SEXUALIZED BY THE MEDIA AND USED IN ADVERTISING CAMPAIGNS. OUR BODIES ARE CONSTANTLY OBJECTIFIED, AND USED AS COMMODITIES THAT MEN PROFIT FROM. WE HAVE NO CHOICE IN HOW OUR BODIES ARE PERCEIVED AND WE ARE CONSTANTLY AVAILABLE FOR PUBLIC VISUAL CONSUMPTION. WE NEED TO FIGHT TO RECLAIM OUR BODIES; WE NEED TO CHALLENGE THE IDEA THAT FEMMES' AND WOMEN'S BODIES ARE SEXUAL OBJECTS TO BE FIGURATIVELY AND LITERALLY BOUGHT AND SOLD; WE NEED TO STAND AGAINST THE PERCEPTION THAT MEN ARE ENTITLED TO WOMEN'S BODIES; AND WE SHOULD WORK ON EMBRACING THE IDEA THAT OUR BODIES BELONG TO US AND US ALONE, THAT THEY WE ARE FREE TO DO WITH THEM WHAT WE PLEASE.

WE PICK UP A LOT OF TOXIC HABITS FROM THE SOCIETAL NORMS OF MONOGAMOUS HETERONORMATIVITY. TAKE THE IDEA THAT JEALOUSY IS AN INDICATION OF LOVE FOR ONE, OR THAT CONFLICT IS A SIGN OF PASSION FOR ANOTHER. MAINSTREAM MEDIA PERPETUATES THESE IDEAS IN THE FILMS AND TELEVISION WE WATCH, DEPICTING COUPLES IN IMPASSIONED RELATIONSHIPS FILLED WITH INTENSE CONFLICT COMBINED WITH VIGOROUS LOVE. RELATIONSHIPS MAY HAVE BOTH CONFLICT AND LOVE, BUT OFTEN THE MEDIA WE CONSUME SUGGESTS THAT THE TWO GO HAND IN HAND AND CAN EVEN NORMALIZE VIOLENCE AND ROMANTICIZE OR GLAMORIZE EMOTIONAL AND PHYSICAL ABUSE. JEALOUSY AND CONFLICT ARE NATURALLY FOUND IN MANY RELATIONSHIPS, AND THEY'RE NOT WRONG OR UNNATURAL, BUT THEY ARE NOT ESSENTIAL TO PASSION, AND THE ABSENCE OF THEM DOES NOT MAKE A RELATIONSHIP PLAIN OR BORING.

JEALOUSY IS NOT AN INDICATION OF LOVE

DISRUPT RAPE CULTURE

RAPE CULTURE REFERS TO THE SPECTRUM OF VIOLENCE THAT WOMEN AND TRANSFEMININE PEOPLE EXPERIENCE IN THEIR DAY-TO-DAY LIVES THAT IS SOCIALLY ACCEPTABLE, BUT SHOULDN'T BE. EVERYTHING FROM SLUT SHAMING, STREET HARASSMENT, VICTIM BLAMING, AND RAPE JOKES TO TRIVIALIZING RAPE, RAPE DENIAL, AND APOLOGISTS ALL ARE PARTS OF RAPE CULTURE AND CONTRIBUTE TO NORMALIZING VIOLENCE AGAINST AND DEHUMANIZING US. LEARN TO IDENTIFY THESE SIGNS OF TOXIC MASCULINITY AND MANIFESTATIONS OF RAPE CULTURE AND ATTEMPT TO DISRUPT THEM WHENEVER YOU CAN. IF YOUR SAFETY IS NOT AT RISK, THEN BE BOLD AND CONFRONT THOSE WHO TELL SEXIST JOKES OR SLUT SHAME; MAKE IT KNOWN THAT THAT BEHAVIOR IS UNACCEPTABLE AND UNCOOL.

SELF-LOVE IS REVOLUTIONARY

THE CAPITALIST PATRIARCHY QUITE LITERALLY BENEFITS FROM YOUR FEELINGS OF INADEQUACY. IT KEEPS YOU SPENDING YOUR MONEY TO "FIX YOURSELF" AND DISTRACTED FROM COMPETING WITH MEN FOR RESOURCES. BY LOVING YOURSELF, YOU ARE CHALLENGING THE DOMINANT POWER STRUCTURES THAT SEEK TO CONTROL YOU. WHEN YOU RESIST, WHEN YOU EXHIBIT INDEPENDENT THOUGHT, YOU EXERCISE YOUR STRENGTH AND YOU ARE REVOLUTIONARY. EACH TIME YOU CHOOSE TO LOVE YOURSELF, EACH TIME YOU CHOOSE TO IGNORE THE EXTERNAL AND INTERNAL VOICES THAT TELL YOU ANYTHING NEGATIVE ABOUT YOURSELF, YOU ARE EXERCISING POWER AND SHOULD BE PROUD OF YOURSELF.

REPRESENTATION IS IMPORTANT

HAVING ROLE MODELS, BEING ABLE TO SEE YOURSELF IN AND IDENTIFY WITH CHARACTERS PRESENTED IN THE MEDIA, IS SO IMPORTANT FOR MANY REASONS. GOOD AND ACCURATE REPRESENTATION HELPS BUILD DREAMS AND GOALS, ALLOWING PEOPLE TO SEE POTENTIAL AND POSSIBILITY IN THEIR LIVES AND IN THEMSELVES. IT IMPROVES SELF-ESTEEM, HELPS WITH SELF-LOVE, AND HELPS PEOPLE FEEL INCLUDED AND LIKE THEIR STORIES ARE IMPORTANT WHEN THEY'RE OFTEN ABSENT. HAVING PROPER REPRESENTATION IS EDUCATIONAL, INSPIRING, AND SIMPLY MORE ACCURATE. PAGING THROUGH THE HISTORY BOOKS TO FIND THAT ALL THE PEOPLE WHO RESEMBLE YOU IN GENDER, RACE, OR SEXUALITY, ETC., HAVE BEEN ERASED, OR EXOTIFIED, IS NOT ONLY WRONG BUT HURTFUL. BE CONSCIOUS AND CRITICAL OF THE REPRESENTATION AROUND YOU AND CELEBRATE THE MEDIA THAT GETS IT RIGHT.

AS WE PREVIOUSLY DISCUSSED, WOMEN'S SEXUALITY IS CONSTANTLY COMMODIFIED FOR CAPITALIST GAIN, OFTEN USED TO SELL PRODUCTS AND SERVICES. HOWEVER, WHEN WOMEN PROJECT IMAGES OF THEMSELVES AS SEXUAL THEY ARE OFTEN CRITICIZED FOR IT, CONSIDERED VAIN, OR EVEN SLUT SHAMED. THIS IS A COMMON AND WICKED DOUBLE STANDARD IN WHICH OUR SOCIETY IS PERFECTLY OKAY WITH SEEING WOMEN'S BODIES SEXUALIZED IN ADVERTISING, BUT ANGERED WHEN WOMEN CLAIM THEIR OWN BODIES, SENSUALITY, AND SEXUALITY. YOU'RE UNIQUE AND WONDERFUL, DON'T BE AFRAID TO POST GORGEOUS PHOTOS OF YOURSELF ON SOCIAL MEDIA IF IT MAKES YOU FEEL GOOD. DON'T BE AFRAID TO EXPRESS YOURSELF, AND WORK ON FEELING MORE COMFORTABLE WITH OWNING YOUR SENSUALITY AND PROJECTING IT INTO THE WORLD.

POST YOUR SELFIES

THERE IS NO SUCH THING
AS "BAD EMOTIONS"

YOU'RE TOLD TO BE STRONG, TO BE BRAVE, TO BE BETTER, BUT SOMETIMES YOU FEEL THE OPPOSITE. DON'T FEEL BAD OR GUILTY ABOUT HAVING NEGATIVE THOUGHTS AND FEELINGS, ESPECIALLY THOSE SOCIETY CONSIDERS TO BE "UGLY," LIKE GUILT AND SHAME. THESE FEELINGS ARE IMPORTANT IN MANY WAYS; THEY REVEAL THINGS ABOUT YOU THAT YOU MAY NOT HAVE BEEN AWARE OF, THEY CAN REMIND YOU OF YOUR HUMANITY AND THE FACT THAT YOU ARE BEAUTIFUL AND BROKEN LIKE WE ALL ARE, AND THEY LEAD TO GROWTH AND LEARNING WHEN YOU INTERROGATE THEM. DO NOT LET THESE FEELINGS STAY BURIED INSIDE YOU, FESTERING AND GROWING IN POWER OVER YOU. RELEASE THEM, SPEAK ABOUT THEM TO THOSE YOU TRUST, GIVE THEM ATTENTION, ACKNOWLEDGE THEM, HONOR THEM, PROCESS THEM, AND THEN LET THEM GO.

DON'T USE ABLEIST SLURS
(ESPECIALLY TO DESCRIBE WOMEN/FEMMES/GENDER-NONCONFORMING PEOPLE)

ABLEISM IS DANGEROUS BECAUSE IT NORMALIZES HARMFUL AND OFFENSIVE LANGUAGE RELATING TO VERY REAL DISABILITIES. ASSOCIATING THE WORD "CRAZY" WITH SOMEONE WHO IS IMPASSIONED IS NOT ONLY REDUCTIVE TO THAT PERSON'S EXPRESSION BUT ALSO MAKES LIGHT OF THOSE SUFFERING DUE TO MENTAL ILLNESS. THIS IS JUST ONE EXAMPLE OF ABLEISM POLLUTING OUR EVERYDAY LANGUAGE.

THERE EXISTS A LONG HISTORY OF ILLEGITIMATING WOMEN'S THOUGHTS, WORDS, ACTIONS, AND FEELINGS THROUGH QUESTIONING THEIR SANITY OR MENTAL HEALTH. WE'RE ALL TOO FAMILIAR WITH THE PHRASES "SHE'S CRAZY" AND "SHE'S INSANE." THE PATRIARCHY UPHOLDS THE IDEA OF A STRICT BINARY WITH SO-CALLED FEMININE QUALITIES VERSUS MASCULINE ONES, "FEMININE" QUALITIES BEING EMOTIONAL, ILLOGICAL, HYSTERICAL, WEAK, IRRATIONAL, ETC., AND "MASCULINE" QUALITIES BEING THE OPPOSITE. SIMILARLY, THERE IS ALSO A LONG HISTORY OF LGBTQ+ PEOPLE'S MENTAL HEALTH BEING CALLED INTO QUESTION. LGBTQ+ FOLKS WERE—AND IN SOME COMMUNITIES STILL ARE—CONSIDERED TO BE "ILL," "BROKEN," AND "IN NEED OF FIXING."

CONTINUED

THERE IS SO MUCH WRONG WITH THESE CONCEPTIONS. FIRST, GENDER IS A SOCIAL CONSTRUCT AND THERE ARE NO PARTICULAR, INHERENT QUALITIES BELONGING TO ANY GENDER. SECOND, THESE NOTIONS ALSO IMPLY THAT SOME FEELINGS OR STATES OF BEING ARE BETTER THAN OTHERS; I.E., THAT LOGIC IS OF HIGHER VALUE THAN EMOTIONAL INTELLIGENCE OR VULNERABILITY. BY USING SEEMINGLY HARMLESS ABLEIST TERMS TO DESCRIBE WOMEN AND TRANSFEMININE PEOPLE, WE REINFORCE THE LONG HISTORY OF OFFENSIVE GENDER-BASED QUALITIES, SUPPORT DANGEROUS STEREOTYPES, AND CONTRIBUTE TO SUPPORTING THE PATRIARCHY.

TRY TO BE CONSCIOUS AND INTENTIONAL WITH WHAT YOU WISH TO SAY AND HOW YOU WISH TO DESCRIBE SOMEONE OR THEIR BEHAVIOR.

INVEST IN YOURSELF

KNOW YOUR POWER

THE WORLD WAS DESIGNED BY AND FOR PEOPLE WITH A PARTICULAR IDENTITY, AND CONSEQUENTLY IT'S MORE DIFFICULT, IN VARYING DEGREES, FOR ALL THE OTHER PEOPLE WHO DON'T SHARE THAT IDENTITY TO NAVIGATE LIFE. KIMBERLÉ CRENSHAW COINED THE TERM *INTERSECTIONALITY* WHEN DESCRIBING THE WAY VARYING FORMS OF OPPRESSION COME TOGETHER TO AFFECT DIFFERENT PEOPLE. WITH WHITE SUPREMACY, CAPITALISM, THE PATRIARCHY, ABELISM, FATPHOBIA, LGBTQ+ PHOBIA, ISLAMAPHOBIA, CLASSISM, MISOGYNY, ANTI-SEMITISM, AND SEXISM, ETC., WIDESPREAD IN OUR WORLD, DEPENDING ON YOUR IDENTITY, ONE OR MORE OF THESE THINGS CONTRIBUTE TOWARD MAKING YOUR LIFE MORE CHALLENGING. BUT DON'T BE DISHEARTENED; YOU HAVE AN IMMENSE CAPACITY TO DISRUPT OPPRESSIVE POWER STRUCTURES AND TO FIGHT INJUSTICE. REALIZE YOUR POWER AND EXERCISE IT; THE MORE YOU DO, THE MORE COMFORTABLE AND CONFIDENT YOU WILL BECOME. EVERY SMALL ACT OF REBELLION COUNTS AND CONTRIBUTES TOWARD A MOVEMENT THAT SEEKS TO CREATE A MORE EQUAL WORLD FOR ALL TO LIVE AND LOVE IN.

WE DON'T HAVE TO BE BEAUTIFUL

SOCIETY HAS SUCH RIDICULOUS STANDARDS FOR WOMEN AND IS OBSESSED WITH US BEING, LOOKING, AND ACTING IN CERTAIN WAYS. WE'RE SUPPOSED TO BEHAVE IN A TAME AND PALATABLE MANNER; TO BE CONFIDENT BUT NOT VAIN, OUTSPOKEN, OR DOMINANT; TO BE FRIENDLY AND SEXUALLY AVAILABLE BUT NOT PROMISCUOUS; TO BE SMART BUT NOT THREATENING.

WE'RE EXPECTED TO ADHERE TO UNREALISTIC BEAUTY STANDARDS THAT ARE COMMUNICATED TO US FROM AN EARLY AGE. MOST OF THE TIME WE ONLY SEE ONE TYPE OF BODY CELEBRATED IN THE WORLD: THAT BEING A WHITE/LIGHT-SKINNED, SLENDER, TALL, SOMETIMES "CURVY," PRETTY, ABLE-BODIED FLAWLESS-FACED, CIS-GENDERED WOMAN OR GIRL. THIS IMAGE CHANGES SLIGHTLY WITH TIME AS FASHION AND TRENDS AFFECT THE "IDEAL LOOK" FOR WOMEN, BUT IT'S ALWAYS THERE, FUELING DISSATISFACTION, AND DISTRACTING US FROM THE MORE IMPORTANT THINGS IN LIFE.

THE TRUTH IS, BEAUTY IS NOT THE MOST IMPORTANT THING IN LIFE. THERE ARE SO MANY MORE IMPORTANT QUALITIES WE ALL HAVE THAT WE CAN GROW

CONTINUED

AND DEVELOP. IT'S DIFFICULT NOT TO BE AFFECTED BY THE INDOCTRINATION OF THE MEDIA; WE ALL HAVE A LOT OF INTERNALIZED DESIRE TO SUBSCRIBE TO BEAUTY STANDARDS, TO FEEL AND TO BE CONSIDERED BEAUTIFUL. LET US TRY TO INTERROGATE AND DISMANTLE THIS DESIRE FOR BEAUTY. LET US CHALLENGE IT WHEN WE COME INTO CONTACT WITH IT. WE ALLOW MEN TO SUCCEED IN LIFE WHEN THEY ARE NOT GOOD-LOOKING. LET US ALLOW WOMEN TO BE UGLY; ALLOW YOURSELF TO BE YOURSELF, ESPECIALLY WHEN YOURSELF IS NOT FEELING OR LOOKING GOOD. YOU ARE CAPABLE OF ACHIEVING SO MUCH AND YOUR LOOKS HAVE GOT VERY LITTLE TO DO WITH WHO YOU ACTUALLY ARE.

GIVE YOURSELF CREDIT

TACKLE YOUR IMPOSTER SYNDROME

IMPOSTER SYNDROME IS THE SENSATION OF BEING A FAKE OR A FRAUD AND HAVING THE CONSTANT INTERNALIZED FEAR THAT ANY DAY YOU'RE GOING TO BE EXPOSED AS THE COUNTERFEIT THAT YOU ARE. THIS IS A VERY REAL PSYCHOLOGICAL PARADIGM AND SO MANY OF US SUFFER FROM IT, PARTICU- LARLY WOMEN AND FEMMES OF COLOR. DO NOT DOUBT YOUR ACHIEVEMENTS AND ACCOMPLISHMENTS, KNOW THAT YOU HAVE ACHIEVED WHAT YOU HAVE BECAUSE YOU ARE COMPETENT AND CAPABLE. TACKLE THOSE FEELINGS OF INADEQUACY AND THAT YOU DON'T BELONG; YOU DO.

WE SPEND OUR LIVES SHAPING OUR IDENTITIES, BEING CONSCIOUS OF THE PEOPLE WE ARE AND HOW WE PROJECT OURSELVES INTO THE WORLD. SOMETIMES WE FIND OURSELVES IN SITUATIONS THAT WE AREN'T COMFORTABLE WITH OR WE FEEL AREN'T RIGHT FOR US—THIS IS TOTALLY FINE AND IT'S GREAT TO BE CONFIDENT ABOUT THE THINGS WE ARE AND AREN'T INTO. HOWEVER, IT'S ALSO GOOD TO NOT BE TOO ATTACHED TO OUR OWN NOTIONS OF OURSELVES; THOSE IDEAS OF THE PERSON WE THINK WE ARE MAY BE HOLDING US BACK. ALLOW YOURSELF TO SURPRISE YOURSELF.

DON'T APOLOGIZE FOR WHO YOU ARE

YOUR FEELINGS ARE VALID

YOU ARE TOUGHER THAN YOU REALIZE

NOBODY HAS THE RIGHT TO DICTATE WHO
OR HOW YOU SHOULD BE

ACKNOWLEDGMENTS

THANK YOU TO MY TEAM AT MORROW GIFT: LIATE STEHLIK, BENJAMIN STEIN-BERG, CASSIE JONES, ANDREA MOLITOR, SUSAN KOSKO, MUMTAZ MUSTAFA, YEON KIM, LEAH CARLSON-STANISIC, BIANCA FLORES, LAUREN LAUZON, TAVIA KOWALCHUK, AND EMMA BRODIE.

AND THANK YOU TO ALL THE WONDERFUL PEOPLE WHO SUBMITTED THEIR PICTURES TO BE ILLUSTRATED FOR THIS BOOK.

YOU ARE MAGIC

HARPERCOLLINS BOOKS MAY BE PURCHASED FOR EDUCATIONAL, BUSINESS, OR SALES PROMOTIONAL USE. FOR INFORMATION, PLEASE EMAIL THE SPECIAL MARKETS DEPARTMENT AT SPSALES@HARPERCOLLINS.COM.

FIRST EDITION

DESIGNED BY LEAH CARLSON-STANISIC

LIBRARY OF CONGRESS CATALOGING-IN-PUBLICATION DATA HAS BEEN APPLIED FOR.

ISBN 978-0-06-286399-7

33614081393695

19 20 21 22 23 SC 10 9 8 7 6 5 4 3 2 1